TRUMP REVEALED

A GREAT PRESIDENT?

KENNETH T. FAIRBANKS

Copyright 2016 by KDM Publishers - All rights reserved.

The following eBook is reproduced below with the goal of providing information that is as accurate and reliable as possible. Regardless, purchasing this eBook can be seen as consent to the fact that both the publisher and the author of this book are in no way experts on the topics discussed within and that any recommendations or suggestions that are made herein are for entertainment purposes only. Professionals should be consulted as needed prior to undertaking any of the action endorsed herein.

This declaration is deemed fair and valid by both the American Bar Association and the Committee of Publishers Association and is legally binding throughout the United States.

Furthermore, the transmission, duplication or reproduction of any of the following work including specific information will be considered an illegal act irrespective of if it is done electronically or in print. This extends to creating a secondary or tertiary copy of the work or a recorded copy and is only allowed with express written consent from the Publisher. All additional right reserved.

The information in the following pages is broadly considered to be a truthful and accurate account of facts and as such any inattention, use or misuse of the information in question by the reader will render any resulting actions solely under their purview. There are no scenarios in which the publisher or the original author of this work can be in any fashion deemed liable for any hardship or damages that may befall them after undertaking information described herein.

Additionally, the information in the following pages is intended only for informational purposes and should thus be thought of as universal. As befitting its nature, it is presented without assurance regarding its prolonged validity or interim quality. Trademarks that are mentioned are done without written consent and can in no way be considered an endorsement from the trademark holder.

INTRODUCTION

Businessman and well-known reality television star Donald Trump announced in 2015 that he would officially take part in the race for the position of the 45th President of the United States. The nation was not sure how to react. Many citizens were sure that this was just a publicity stunt, that a man with no history in politics would actually consider running for President; while others were excited about the fact that our country may again have a leader, who could not be so easily bought off as other, more "traditional", politicians had.

Donald Trump had an exciting campaign for the presidency: from his investigation and instigating of opponent Hillary Clinton to his seemingly never-ending promises for success post election.

In *Trump Revealed: A Great President?* we will first offer a short biography of who the 45th President of the United States is, followed by facts about his Presidential campaign trail, Trump's goals for the 45th presidency, the election results of the 2016 presidential election, and what was accomplished during Donald Trump's first year in office as the United States of America's 45th President.

Trump Revealed: A Great President? offers a neutral position to the Trump Presidency, evaluating his presidency from an objective standpoint that is neither "pro-Trump" or "anti-Trump", so that you may decide for yourself answers to the following questions:

- Is Donald J. Trump truly working for the American people or just working towards benefiting his own personal legacy?

- Is Donald Trump taking the presidency seriously or is this position of power the result of a publicity stunt gone too far?

- What was Donald Trump trying to prove on the campaign trail? What is he trying to achieve in office? Has he achieved some of his goals while holding office as the 45th President of the United States of America?

So, you decide: is President Donald J. Trump working hard to represent the American people, or is he simply holding this position of power to benefit his own personal legacy? Is Donald Trump treating this position of office seriously or was this really just a publicity stunt gone too far? What do you believe Donald Trump was trying to achieve in running for President, and has he achieved any or all of his goals in the White House? And lastly, is Donald Trump really doing as he promised and making America great again?

1

WHO IS DONALD JOHN TRUMP?

You have to think anyway, so why not think big?

— DONALD TRUMP

DONALD JOHN TRUMP was born in New York on June 14, 1946. Donald Trump was born to proud parents: father Fred Trump (an established real estate tycoon) and Mary Anne McLeod (a woman who immigrated from her native country of Scotland in the year 1929).

TRUMP GRADUATED from the University of Pennsylvania's Wharton School of Finance in 1968, obtaining a degree in economics. Since graduation from college, Donald Trump continued to succeed and grow to be both a well-known businessman and reality television star.

In 1989, Milton Bradley released a *Trump* board game that never amounted to much, the board game was obviously not as successful as Donald Trump's other business ventures or his political aspirations.

Donald Trump first met Melania during New York fashion week, at a party, in 1998. At the party, Melania reportedly did not give Trump her phone number, though he left his with her and she called him later on. In 1999, Donald Trump described his then girlfriend Melania as being "first lady material" during a phone call to the Howard Stern show. Donald Trump and Melania broke up for a brief period in the year 2000 (just before Trump's short lived first run for President) but were reunited as a couple again shortly after their separation. In the summer of 2002, Donald met Melania's parents for the first time in her native Slovenia. Donald Trump proposed marriage to Melania in 2004, and the pair were married in the year 2005 (with Bill and Hillary Clinton attending the wedding as guests). Barron Trump, son to Donald and Melania, was born in 2006.

Also in the year 2006, Donald Trump released Trump Vodka, though he does not personally drink alcohol (a habit in which he does not partake because his brother, Fred Trump Jr., died of alcoholism in 1981).

In 2012, rumors circulated that Donald Trump may run for President of the United States, though nothing came of these rumors then. In 2015, however, Donald Trump officially announced his candidacy for the 45th President of the United States. Donald Trump accepted the Presidential nomination by the Republican National Convention on July 21, 2016 and, as a result, was elected to the position of President in November 2016. Among his many campaign promises on what to expect as national progress from his Presidency were a near elimination of violence in America, a no tolerance stance against terrorism, an improvement in the nation's economy, and a tough stance against illegal immigration. Check in with chapter five of *Trump Revealed: A Great Presidency?* to see which of his campaign goals were focused on or achieved during Donald Trump's first year in office.

2

TRUMP'S CAMPAIGN TRAIL

I think apologizing's a great thing, but you have to be wrong. I will absolutely apologize, sometime in the hopefully distant future, if I'm ever wrong.

— DONALD TRUMP

"MAKE AMERICA GREAT AGAIN", is the campaign slogan that took the nation by storm. This simple phrase gave hope for the future to thousands of Americans who, naturally, only wanted the best for the country in which they reside. This slogan could be seen on clothing and apparel, as well as heard being chanted at each of Trump's campaign rallies. But where did the campaign begin?

Many people may consider November 2016, and more specifically November 8, to be the start of Donald Trump's political career. After all, that was the day that he was elected to be the 45th President of The

United States of America, and he had no prior political experience. Some think that his race for presidential office started long before he announced his candidacy in 2015, however, at the White House Correspondents' Dinner (held in April 2011).

In April of 2011, Donald Trump attended the White House Correspondents' Dinner as a guest of The Washington Post. What had promised to be an eventful, pleasant evening reportedly ended with Donald Trump being quite embarrassed by personal and political jabs made by then President Barack Obama and comedian Seth Meyers. Barack Obama attacked Trump's television career and criticized any interest the future presidential candidate had in politics, while American comedian Seth Meyers joked,

"Donald Trump has been saying that he will run for President as a Republican, which is surprising since I just assumed that he was running as a joke".

Many believe that the personal criticisms and embarrassment that occurred at the White House Correspondents' Dinner in 2011 spurred Donald Trump to run for President if only to gain stature or to simply "prove a point" about his political capabilities. After all, what better way to be taken seriously politically than to hold office as the 45th President of the United States of America?

Salon.com's Amanda Marcotte is quoted in stating that *"...the evidence is pointing to a certain conclusion: Donald Trump is running for President because he believes the power and fame of the White House will allow him to settle the score in his ever-expanding list of petty grievances".*

Donald Trump officially announced his candidacy for the 2016 Presidential election in 2015. Trump listed his goals for the presidency to range from fighting violence in America and terrorism to strengthening the economy and fighting immigration; all while denying allegations that his run for office was a publicity stunt, to "gain stature", or to prove a point. Trump has stated numerous times that he can handle criticism, and that the White House Correspondents' Dinner in 2011 did not play a role in his decision to participate in the 2016 presidential election.

Donald Trump has been asked if his run for the American presidency was a result of him seeking additional fame, and he has repeatedly stated that that is not the case. When directly asked why he decided to run as a candidate in the 2016 presidential election, he answered simply "I had to do it for myself" (elaborating that he did not want to look back in 10 years and wonder what he could have accomplished or recognize what he could have but didn't give himself the chance to).

One could use Trump's presidential salary, or lack thereof, as proof that he is not simply holding the most highly respected political office in our country for personal gain. Donald Trump refused to collect a presidential salary, and subsequently donated his first quarter's salary of roughly $78,000 to the National Parks Service (NPS) to repair historic battlefields. Donald Trump's second quarter salary contributed to a donation of $100,000 to the Department of Education (Education Secretary Betsy DeVos).

During his campaign for office Trump swore he would not accept a presidential salary while in office, a promise that he has since kept. Has he kept his other campaign promises? Listed below are some of Donald Trump's most well-known campaign promises, and chapter four of *Trump Revealed: A Great President?* will evaluate which of his campaign promises he has dedicated the most effort to keeping during his first year in office.

- To build a border wall between the United States and Mexico (and make Mexico fund the project).

- Fully repeal Obamacare and replace it with a fairer and market based alternative health care system.

- Temporarily ban Muslim immigrants from entering the United States.

- "Drain the Swamp" of bureaucracy in Washington (likely taken from the phrase used by President Ronald Reagan).

President Donald Trump also saw numerous conflicts, tragedies, and criticisms his first year in the Oval Office (as any president surely does). Chapter 5 of *Trump Revealed: A Great President?* will display the challenges that President Donald Trump faced in his first year in office as well as how he addressed and resolved the issues placed before him.

3

ELECTION RESULTS 2016

If voting made any difference they wouldn't let us do it.

— MARK TWAIN

DONALD JOHN TRUMP tweeted out the above statement at 5:43 AM on November 8, 2016 (the morning of the 2016 presidential election). Trump seemed confident that he would win the 2016 election, and promised the American people that his position in office would result in overall success for the country in which we live.

ON NOVEMBER 8, 2016 more than 126 million people went to the polls and cast their vote for who they thought should be the 45th President of the United States of America. While the final votes tallied to be roughly 128 million total votes cast, this only accounted for roughly 55% of eligible voters in the United States.

Citizens cast their votes and then had nothing to do but wait. Watching the news or listening to the radio, the same question was on nearly everyone's mind that day: what would the results of the 2016 presidential election be? Who would become the 45th President of the United States of America?

The results were announced late that evening: Donald J. Trump had won the 2016 election, and was now named the 45th President of the United States. As the final count for the votes came in, America learned that Donald Trump had won the electoral college votes by a landslide, though he lost the popular vote by nearly 3 million votes (a fact that outraged a portion of the nation).

To take office as President, a candidate needs to obtain 270 votes from the electoral college. In the 2016 Presidential election, Donald J. Trump obtained 306 electoral votes (26 more than Hillary Clinton's 232 electoral votes). Donald Trump also won 30 states, 10 more than Hillary's 20 states in the 2016 presidential election.

The popular vote was not as close as the electoral vote: Trump won 46.4% of the popular vote with 62,984,825 votes against Hillary's vote total of 65,853,516, or 48.5%.

(Official vote statistics taken from www.cnn.com/election/results).

UPON LEARNING the results of the 2016 Presidential election on that Tuesday night, Hillary Clinton failed to make an appearance and would not speak to the thousands of supporters who had come to the Javits Center to show their support. She appeared the following day at the New Yorker Hotel to deliver her concession speech instead, leaving many of her supporters disappointed.

DONALD TRUMP HOWEVER, had a very different evening signifying the end of the 2016 presidential election. Below are a few quotes taken from Donald Trump's acceptance speech given early in the morning on November 9, 2016:

"WE HAVE TO GET TOGETHER. *I say it is time for us together as one united people*"

"WE WILL BEGIN *the urgent task of renewing the American dream*"

"THE FORGOTTEN AMERICAN *will be forgotten no longer*"

"TO BE TRULY *historic we have to do a great job, and I promise you I will not let you down*"

"YOU WILL BE *proud of your President, I love this country*"

PRESIDENT DONALD TRUMP'S acceptance speech confirmed the reason that millions of Americans cast their vote for him in the 2016 presidential election: his acceptance speech conveyed a sense of pride in America, and he repeatedly stated that the citizens of the United States must unite in order for the United States to move forward successfully. During his campaign for presidency, Donald Trump repeatedly stated that he would work to represent the "average American" and that the result would be a country that all of our citizens would again to proud to reside in and be a part of: for millions of Americans, this was one of the main reasons for voting for Trump, and it was a sort of relief to hear he planned to keep his word moving forward into the presidency.

LIKE ALL PRESIDENTIAL CANDIDATES DO, Donald Trump made a lot of promises and outlined a lot of goals during his campaign for the presidency. After his election, Americans could do little more than wait and see how many of these promises would be kept and wonder how our country would be transformed in the years to come.

THE ABOVE TWEET was released in the early hours of November 9, 2016 after the results of the 2016 presidential election had been learnt.

DONALD TRUMP'S election to the position of the 45th President of the United States saw a wide spread display of reactions from people all around the world. Some still thought this was a joke gone too far, while Trump's thousands of supporters voiced their excitement in having a President with no political background that had promised to advocate for the "average" American throughout his Presidency. Almost immediately after his election in 2016, many Trump supporters had already began advocating for his reelection for a second term in 2020.

Donald Trump faced a good deal of celebrity criticism throughout his campaign for presidency, and this did not stop after his election. At 1AM on November 9, 2016 Lady Gaga tweeted "say a prayer America", while Family Guy creator and comedian Seth MacFarlane tweeted "I truly cannot visualize the rambling, incoherent creature I saw at the debates now addressing the nation from the Oval Office".

Donald Trump's campaign trail saw almost unlimited backlash and criticism, though that didn't seem to slow his momentum moving forward towards his goal of becoming the 45th President of the United States. Whether you agreed with his past, his politics, or his sometimes-tactless statements or not; one thing was decided: the American people had spoken, and they were ready to "Make America Great Again!".

4

GOALS FOR THE 45TH PRESIDENCY

> The wall will be ten feet taller. And every time they protest, it's going to go up a little bit higher.
>
> — DONALD TRUMP

PRESIDENT DONALD TRUMP'S four most commonly discussed goals for his presidency are listed below:
- To build a border wall between the United States and Mexico (and make Mexico fund the project).
- Fully repeal Obamacare and replace it with a fairer and market based alternative health care system.
- Temporarily ban Muslim immigrants from entering the United States.
- "Drain the Swamp" of bureaucracy in Washington (likely taken from the phrase used by President Ronald Reagan).

Has Donald Trump kept these campaign promises? Was Donald J.

Trump serious during his campaign for President, is he serious about being an influential political figure or were these just empty promises made to gain more attention? Below we evaluate, from a purely objective standpoint, the campaign promises he made and if any progress has been made to see each become a reality.

Building A Border Wall Between the United States and Mexico

One of Donald Trump's most often discussed campaign goals was the promise to build a border wall between the United States and Mexico. Donald Trump and his supporters hoped that such a wall would nearly halt the illegal entry of immigrants into the United States from Mexico. During his campaign, real estate developer and presidential nominee Trump had promised that he *"...would build a great wall, and nobody builds walls better than me"*. This quote did not take anyone by surprise, as Trump's repeated promise for a border wall to stop illegal immigration was promised throughout his campaign for the presidency. His official stance on immigration could seemingly be summed up in another quote of his: "We are going to build a great border wall to stop illegal immigration, to stop the gangs and the violence, and to stop the drugs from pouring into our communities."

It seemed that Trump was completely serious about the construction of a border wall between the United States and Mexico, and he made multiple claims that the construction of a border wall would help in the resolution of other problems such as violence in the United States and the ever-growing drug trade. So almost a full year into his presidency, what has come of the "great border wall"? What, if anything, has been done to accomplish this popular campaign promise?

After his election, many rumored that the construction of a border wall between the United States and Mexico was unrealistic and simply would not happen. Even if a border wall was to be constructed, Mexico would not possibly be footing the bill. Right?

On September 26, 2017 Customs Border Patrol (CBP) tweeted a message that "Construction of eight wall prototypes began today in San Diego. The prototypes are designed to deter illegal border crossings". So, while the construction of a border wall between the United States and Mexico was not an immediately kept campaign promise, it seems that it was not a lie nor was it simply "swept under the rug" and it could one day soon be a very real project.

Much to the delight of many American citizens, President Donald Trump's plan to construct a border wall between the United States and Mexico seemed to have garnered some support from Israel's Prime Minister Benjamin Netanyahu:

As for payment of the border wall: President Donald Trump states that while he is aware that Mexico will never cut a check for the construction of the wall, any costs accumulated in constructing the border wall will be deducted from any aid that would be given to Mexico from the United States, resulting in Mexico's indirect payment for the wall.

The above tweet garnered some backlash because, to some, it seems to imply that the vast majority of Mexican immigrants are rapists or criminals. While this would surely be cause for outrage if it were true, many argue that President Trump was not generalizing a whole nation's citizens: that to do so would in fact be racist but this was not the case. Trump supporters argue that the President is merely trying to eliminate the 27% of prisoners in federal prisons that consist of criminal aliens (statistic taken from heritage.org) (criminal activity and crimes that would not have been committed if the United States had tougher immigration laws and restrictions in place). One of Donald Trump's biggest discussion points during his campaign was trying to eliminate terrorism from foreign nations in the United

States, so it made sense that he would (at least temporarily) attempt to control immigration as a safety precaution.

Fully Repeal "Obamacare"

Another of President Trump's popular campaign promises was to fully repeal the Affordable Care Act (ACA), otherwise known as Obamacare. The Affordable Care Act required American citizens to choose and purchase a health insurance plan from the United States government, refusal to do so would result in an annual monetary fine until they enrolled in a government regulated healthcare plan.

While a large number of American citizens are against the Affordable Care Act's mandate to purchase a health insurance plan, sometimes imposing unrealistic premiums upon the patient, there is still the concern of how Obamacare could realistically be fully repealed as well as the worry of what the government could come up with as a replacement plan. Eleven months into Donald Trump's presidency, where do we stand on repealing Obamacare? Has any progress been made in improving the healthcare system for American citizens? The answer, yes but baby steps.

Republican senators proposed a new government healthcare plan to replace, rather than completely repeal, the Affordable Care Act enacted during Barack Obama's Presidency. The newly proposed and revised healthcare bill named the Better Care Reconciliation Act had already passed by the House of Representatives and had numerous changes from the Affordable Care Act. One of the major changes was that American citizens were no longer required to pay a tax penalty for not having health insurance, instead they would only face a thirty percent surcharge on annual insurance premiums if they chose to go without health coverage for more than 63 days. The Better Care Reconciliation Act completely repealed the portion of Obamacare which required any company with more than fifty employees to offer health insurance (facing a penalty if they do not comply). One mandate set in place by Obamacare that would remain unchanged under The Better Care

Reconciliation Act is the requirement for health insurers to allow parents to keep their children on their health insurance policies until those children reach the age of 26. Perhaps one of the major changes between the Affordable Care Act and The Better Care Reconciliation Act is shown in what would now be required as coverage under the newly proposed health plan. Obamacare required all health plans to cover certain services such as yearly physical exams, maternity coverage, emergency room visits, and cancer treatments: The Better Care Reconciliation Act would allow health insurers to offer "bare bones" health plans, that would allow people to have health coverage while paying much lower premiums, so long as at least one of their health plans continues to comply with Obamacare rules concerning essential coverage/benefits.

While many Americans disliked the mandate to purchase healthcare from the government and looked forward to Obamacare being repealed, finding a replacement healthcare system for the American people was found to be a more difficult task than was originally thought.

Placing a Temporary Travel Ban on Muslims

Two of Donald Trump's most common discussion points on the campaign trail were building a border wall and greatly reducing terrorism within the United States (specifically, placing a temporary travel ban on Muslims so that they could no longer enter the United States). The progress of the promised "great wall" has already been discussed, but it is easy to overlook any efforts that President Donald Trump has made in order to restrict immigration in an effort to eliminate terrorism in the United States. There have been multiple executive orders and travel bans put in place during Donald Trump's first year in office, each one modified slightly from the one before it. Below is a compilation of the travel bans that have been put in place during 2017 in the format of a summarized timeline:

- January 27, 2017: Donald Trump issued an executive order that banned the entry of people from Iraq, Yemen, Somalia, Sudan, Iran, Libya, and Syria for 3 months. This travel ban spurred protests at multiple airports nationwide almost immediately. On January 30, 2017 President Donald Trump fired Attorney General Sally Yates for refusing to defend the travel ban. On February 2, the Trump administration became more flexible on the travel ban's restrictions for citizens holding green cards.

- March 6, 2017: President Donald Trump revealed a newly revised travel ban that would exclude immigrants from Iraq moving forward. The travel ban would become effective on March 16 and would continue to temporarily ban the entry of citizens from Yemen, Somalia, Syria, Sudan, Iran, and Libya for 3 months (also banning all refugees for 4 months).

"Drain the Swamp"

During Donald Trump's campaign for the 2016 presidential election, he could often be heard discussing that it was time for America to "drain the swamp" of dishonest and corrupt politicians holding positions of political power in Washington. Trump is quoted in stating "It is time to drain the swamp in Washington, D.C. This is why I'm proposing a package of ethics reforms to make our government honest once again" at one of his rallies in Wisconsin. Trump has held fast and true to his promise to "drain the swamp" in Washington and has made several steps to be sure this continues. In January 2017, Trump issued an executive order: a revolving door ban with a five-year limit for those he appointed, this kept political officials from leaving their careers in government and subsequently lobbying their former colleagues. The executive order set in place by President Donald Trump also imposed a lifetime ban for any senior executive branch official for lobbying for a foreign government.

5

PRESIDENT TRUMP'S FIRST YEAR

The president and a small group of people know exactly what he meant.

— SEAN SPICER

WHETHER DONALD TRUMP decided to run for President of The United States as a joke or not, he was elected in November 2016. During his first year of presidency, Donald Trump has faced numerous problems and tragedies both political and non. His use of Twitter to convey information to the American people is noted as a first by most citizens, and has helped him make quick, personal statements at times of national uncertainty (after natural disasters, mass shootings, etc.).

DONALD TRUMP'S **Use of Twitter**

Since the beginning of his campaign for the 2016 presidential election, Donald Trump has utilized the social media platform Twitter to convey statements and plans to his supporters. Donald Trump is not the first President to utilize modern technology platforms in order to connect with the American people: Franklin Delano Roosevelt utilized the radio (moderately new technology at the time) in order to stay connected with the American people and ease tensions during his "fireside chats". Donald Trump's use of a social media platform to release statements and remarks has been criticized by many as being unprofessional and immature, however it can be viewed as an intelligent move when thought through. A great portion of America is relatively uneducated on political issues. In 2017, most people do not have time to attend political rallies or disrupt their schedules to watch candidates make speeches on the evening news. The use of a social media platform allows voters to stay educated on their candidate's plans for presidency. According to a poll taken by USA Today in July 2017, 67% of American citizens disapprove of President Donald Trump's regular use of Twitter, though his main Twitter account had 32.4 million followers in June 2017.

The Right to Take a Knee

All American citizens have the right to peaceful protest in the United States, though it was demonstrated in 2017 how this basic right can quickly rile up many of the nation's citizens. During the

2016 NFL (National Football League) season, Colin Kaepernick (quarterback for the San Francisco 49ers) made the choice to kneel during the playing of the national anthem in order to protest "injustices faced by people of color, particularly at the hands of police officers". This choice was widely unpopular with American citizens, and Kaepernick gained a fair amount of backlash for it. In 2017, President Donald Trump publicly criticized any NFL player who chose to kneel for the playing of the national anthem. This criticism had a wide range of reactions: NFL team owners, coaches, and players criticized Donald Trump and claimed that this was the President's attempt to restrict their rights to peaceful protest as American citizens. Most Americans however, agreed with President Donald Trump that to kneel during the national anthem was to show great disrespect for the anthem, our flag, and our military. Diane Hessan surveyed 400 voters in December 2016 and found that more than 40% of those participating disagreed with Colin Kaepernick and sided with President Donald Trump on the issue.

PRESIDENT DONALD TRUMP released a series of tweets restating his stance on the matter of kneeling during the national anthem as a way to engage in peaceful protest: citing that to do so was not a way to protest racial inequality but was simply disrespectful to our national anthem, our country, our flag, and our military.

ONE ISSUE SITED by American citizens during the argument of taking a knee during the playing of the national anthem was the following: in July 2016 the Dallas Cowboys wanted to support the Dallas police officers by wearing a simple decal, however they were told that that display of activism was banned. Many consider it to be simple hypocrisy to say that an NFL football player cannot wear a decal supporting police officers but for coaches to say it is their right to kneel during the anthem as an act of protest.

AN ACTIVE HURRICANE Season

2017 saw a very active and surely destructive hurricane season. Hurricane season 2017 has seen such destruction, and has even set a record (though it's not one to be excited about): 2017 was the first year to have three Category 4 hurricanes hit the United States in the same year. The United States saw back to back category 4 hurricanes Harvey, Irma, and Maria; causing major flooding and destruction in Texas, Florida, and southern states. As of October 2017: hurricane Harvey had claimed 75 lives (mostly in the state of Texas), hurricane Irma had taken 87 lives in the United States, while hurricane Maria had currently taken 34 lives in Puerto Rico. As of October 2017, eight hurricanes had formed so far which is still far less than the reported 15 hurricanes of 2005.

HOW DID President Donald Trump handle such an active hurricane season? Donald Trump urged American citizens in southern states to prepare and stay safe during the 2017 hurricane season, and continually tweeted and verbally stated his support for our country's citizens in dealing with the destruction caused by the major storm systems. President Donald Trump saw to it that federal aid was available almost immediately after major hurricanes hit Florida and Texas in the late summer of 2017, and asked Congress for $29 billion for disaster relief funds after visiting Puerto Rico in October of 2017.

PRESIDENT DONALD TRUMP has stated that he does not believe that climate change is necessarily responsible for the more active and destructive hurricane season experienced by the United States in 2017. On a lighter note, a tweet on global warming from Donald Trump in March 2013:

Fake News

Everyone knows you cannot always believe what you hear or see, especially with the internet bringing false information right to your fingertips. It has also long been known that the media tends to dramatize events or "stretch the truth" to gain ratings. The topic of "fake news" has been an issue throughout Donald Trump's presidential campaign as well as the first year of his presidency. President Donald Trump has even released multiple tweets on the subject:

WHILE SOME CRITICIZE that President Donald Trump will claim that anything criticizing his actions to be "fake news", others agree that some media and news outlets such as CNN, NBC, and ABC report questionable news stories in an attempt to spread dislike for the 45th President of the United States.

SEVERAL NEWS OUTLETS have claimed that Donald Trump, his son, and/or his associates have had secret dealings with representatives from Russia through his first year of presidency; causing skepticism and disapproval from the American people who fear for national safety. In September 2017, President Donald Trump urged the Senate committee to perform an investigation into some of the allegedly generated "fake news" concerning the matter. Richard Burr (Senate Intelligence Chairman) agreed to investigate and "present the facts" and stated that news organizations who generated fake news at the expense of the American government would be held "accountable" for their false reporting. Burr states that the Senate was *"...not investigating news organizations - holding them accountable for what they say with no sources to substantiate the facts".*

"Covfefe" **Anyone?**

Shortly after midnight on May 31, 2017 President Donald Trump released the above tweet. Thousands of people waited for the tweet to be deleted, as surely "covfefe" was a typo and at least the President would notice and correct the error. It was later determined that the tweet was to be about fake news article and the constant negative press COVERAGE (not covfefe), though this point was not elaborated on for some time. Meanwhile, thousands of followers watched and waited for the tweet to be deleted or corrected. When no correction came, the news of "covfefe" spread like wildfire, generating dozens of jokes along the way. Hundreds vowed to order an extra-large "covfefe" at Starbucks on their way to work that morning, others were quite sure that the President was exhausted and badly need a cup of "covfefe" when typing the above tweet. However, when the correction did come, it was not as expected. Rather than editing or deleting the tweet, the President displayed a good sense of humor and joined in on the jokes with the tweet displayed below:

AFTERWORD

When Donald J. Trump announced in 2015 that he planned to run in the presidential election the following year, the citizens of the United States had mixed feelings about how to react. Some felt that he was not adequately qualified to hold such a respected position, some felt that surely this must be some sort of joke or publicity stunt, and others were thrilled at the idea of being represented by a "real American" rather than a "traditional" politician.

Thousands of American citizens were sure that Donald Trump was only seeking to hold office as the 45th President of The United States of America to gain stature or benefit his own personal legacy, though Trump refused to collect a presidential salary and even donated his first quarter's presidential salary to the National Park Service.

Trump made many campaign promises for what would be achieved during the 45th presidency of the United States should he be elected, and *Trump Revealed: A Great President?* has taken a look back at those campaign promises as well as what kind of progress, if any, has been made into keeping them. *Trump Revealed: A Great President?* has offered a neutral position to these issues so that you may decide for yourself what kind of leader Donald John Trump has been for the citizens of The United States of America.

While trying to keep his many campaign promises such as fighting terrorism in the US, boosting the economy, and building a border wall; Donald J. Trump also faced many challenges during his first year as the 45th President of The United States (such as a very active and destructive hurricane season, fake news outlets, and many of the nation's athletes engaging in their right to peaceful protest during the national anthem). There is a common phrase *"It's not what happens, it's how you handle it"* that can be used in evaluating Donald Trump's choices as President. He certainly had a lot happen in his first year in office, from conquering the racial divide to trying to keep the nation hopeful for the future after a mass shooting: but how did he handle these events? Great Presidents are not defined by what happens to our nation while they are in office, but rather how they address the American people that they have been elected to lead and how they resolve the many challenges and conflicts that they face.

So, you decide: is President Donald J. Trump working hard to represent the American people, or is he simply holding this position of power to benefit his own personal legacy? Is Donald Trump treating this position of office seriously or was this really just a publicity stunt gone too far? What do you believe Donald Trump was trying to achieve in running for President, and has he achieved any or all of his goals in the White House?

Manufactured by Amazon.ca
Acheson, AB

16072250R00024